Christchurch

in old picture postcards volume 2

by Sue Newman

European Library ZALTBOMMEL/THE NETHERLANDS

 GB ISBN 90 288 6395 8

© 1997 European Library – Zaltbommel/The Netherlands

Introduction

Christchurch is 'somewhat straggling, built without compactness, and with very little regard to architectural taste, although recent improvements have done much to redeem its character in this particular, and various buildings have been erected, giving it a more modern appearance'. So says a guide to the town of 1867, leaving us somewhat bemused from a contemporary point of view. This writer could not foresee the effect of this continuing process of modernisation that has changed so much of Christchurch – but not all – since the last war. However, attitudes also change, and that opinion of 130 years ago would not accord with today's assessment of our charming but crowded town – or what is left of it after the modernisation process referred to above has accelerated beyond the wildest expectations of our Victorian forbears. That the town was straggling is certainly true: at the north-western end in the Stour valley it commenced with humble cottages on St Catherine's Hill and Fairmile; continued through Bargates into the High Street (the 'Cow Street' of medieval days), from which a short cul-de-sac branched off to the Priory Church ('a triumph of architectural taste', enthuses our guide); on down Castle Street and on to its continuation, Bridge Street; on without pause through Purewell from where a sharp turn is made into Stanpit, which leads into Mudeford. At the time of the publication of our guide, that was Christchurch, more or less. Highcliffe was just a disregarded

place only a little earlier known without affectation as Slop Pond. The thinly inhabited, rural settlement of Christchurch had little satellite outposts: Iford village, Wick village, and Tuckton village amongst them – all now suburbs of Bournemouth. And this insignificant and strung-out town was set amidst a vast, seemingly endless stretch of wild heath and woodland.

The opinion of this town had barely improved nearly just fifty years further on. 'Poor old Christchurch,' commences a letter in the local paper in 1916. 'Such a long time dying'. Our newly arrived correspondent, whilst accepting that the town was surrounded by 'charming lanes, meadows and forests; fine, breezy moors and two grand rivers for boating or fishing,' with 'glorious views from St Catherine's Hill', goes on to despair of the town itself on closer acquaintance. 'Most of the town's beauties,' he says, 'are superficial, imaginary, or very exaggerated.' After this unwelcome slur, he comes to the point: 'The natural grandeur remains, but everything made by man is decadent.' His particular bone of contention was the newly-arrived and 'abominable' trams, and 'other motor monstrosities'. How we can sympathise, yet still envy from our distance in time the era when only a rumbling tram or the odd, quaint 'motor car' blighted the peace! We understand this criticism, perhaps: it is the high price we pay for living in modern – and we think, better – times. But the anonymous correspondent's other complaints – the 'Slough of Despond' at the Quay; with its 'number-less rubbish heaps'; the 'dismal swamp' of Quomps' and the 'old broken crockery, tins and bottles' which greeted the eye on a glance down at the river from the medieval Town Bridge, are, thankfully, part of the past we would not wish to revive. 'A large number of houses are just melting away; grass and herbage grows on the roof and walls, giving an already ugly street a ... confessional sort of appearance,' continues our unhappy observer, before deriding the hapless principal inhabitants for being responsible for the 'attenuated, weary, washed-out, woe-begone appearance of the whole town'. 'All we want,' he concludes, 'is a few men of push and go who are not suffering from cranial obesity,' and all will be well – and Christchurch can be made as beautiful as Bournemouth, he ends, somewhat controversially.

Look at the pictures in this volume, and judge for yourself the qualities of our overgrown but still admired town. Without being in any way unfair to our enormous neighbour, which swallowed up so much Christchurch territory in the period from which these pictures are drawn, we must treasure what remains of our ancient, but no longer antiquated, quiet, but no longer sleepy, charming town. We can boast no less than six buildings which are so architecturally and historically important that they merit the select Grade 1 status, numerous build-ings of Grade 11 or 11* status, several Scheduled Ancient Monuments and twelve Conservation Areas, demonstrating that present-day observers, in a world of relentless and often faceless development, make a very different judgement of the town we are fortunate to inhabit or visit.

Acknowledgements

To the contributors: Alan Ivamy, Betty Tompkin, John Lewis, Mabel Norman, the late Allen White, Mike and Wendy Tizzard, Fred Dixon, Brian Sherry, Ada Cutler, Ann White, Ted Davey, Ken Morgan, Nigel Brown, Sally Hall, Peter Jenkins, and the author. Illustrations numbered 13, 15, 16, and 17 are from the collection of the Christchurch Local History Society. Illustrations numbered 5, 9, 12, and 14 appear by kind permission of the Hampshire County Council's Allen White Collection in the Red House Museum, Christchurch. Illustrations numbered 18, 20, 21, 22, 23, 38, 40, 48, 51, 55, 64, 65 and 75 appear by the kind permission of Christchurch Borough Council. Illustration number 46 appears with the permission of Classic Cards of Christchurch.

1   In the first few years of the twentieth century, a climb to the top of the Priory tower would reward you with this view of the small town of Christchurch spread out below, winding along the High Street and Bargates but soon disappearing in a rural hinterland which creeps up to the very edge of the narrow streets. In the foreground, at the corner of Church Lane and Church Street, is Alfred Mallett's Priory Studio, a well-known local photographer who published some of the postcards included in this book. A little way behind it can be seen the roof of the Square House, whilst in the far distant left steam billows from the aptly named Christchurch Steam Brewery.

Note the pony and trap turning the corner of the High Street into Castle Street. In the far distance, St Catherine's Hill looks down on the little town from the other direction.

CHRISTCHURCH. — View from Tower of Christchurch Priory. — LL.

2   The most familiar of the many beauty spots in the town, the quay at the time of this postcard was a muddy landing stage; on the extreme left the common land known as Quomps was until the level was raised in 1912 no more than a swamp. The original parish workhouse, at the time of the photograph used as a private family house but now the Red House Museum, is visible on the left with the vicarage just beyond. In front of the church can be seen a survivor of the pre-Reformation monastery buildings. Next to it is the home of the miller for Place Mill and to the right a glimpse of Priory House, built behind the Priory in the late eighteenth century. Pleasure craft fill the foreground of the picture: the days when shallow-draughted barges could deliver coal and other goods at the Quay having recently come to an end.

Christchurch. The Priory from the Stour.

3 A lucrative but not always reliable living has for centuries been earned by Christchurch fishermen in the salmon season, using either draught nets cast from boats or rod and line. Local salmon, an especially highly regarded delicacy, fetched high prices on the London markets. But the catches vary: in 1880, a 52lb specimen was caught in the Run at Mudeford, centre of the industry. The men wore a 'barble', or leather apron, leather sleeves, and carried a 'knocker' for killing the salmon. During the nineteenth century the catches almost continually declined, which was blamed on an alteration in the course of the Stour river. The season extended from early February until early June.

Salmon Fishing.   near Christchurch.

4 'Cars are requested not to stand beyond this notice-board,' politely requests the sign on the right. Church Street had by this date, about the early 1920s, become the nucleus of a burgeoning tourist industry, and capitalised with a plethora of teashops, although the building which today boasts the Splinters Restaurant seems to be a private house still. On the right a sign proclaims the premises of the Christchurch Art Workers. Now known as the Eight Bells gift shop, at the time of this postcard it was the centre for art exhibitions, displays of furniture and pottery, handweaving, leatherwork and other crafts. Note the sign on the left advertising Judges' postcards, highly regarded for their quality then as now. At the end of Church Street an avenue of elm trees lines the stone-paved approach to the Priory Church porch.

Church Street, Christchurch

5 An early view of the High Street from the junction with Church Street and Castle Street. Dated 1875, it shows it only partially converted to commercial use. In 1870 there were only about 35 shops in these three streets, but the population of the entire parish was only just over 7,000 in 1861 (and this included part of modern Bournemouth). At the extreme left is a glimpse of the brewery, next to which are the premises of George Ferrey, draper and tailor, which was rebuilt in 1899 and now has three storeys. Opposite are the corner premises of Number 2 High Street, ground-floor frontage intact. The photographer was one William Pousty, who operated from a mobile (horse-drawn) vehicle. He left Christchurch in 1882 in search of a better life in Tasmania, but left us with a record of a quiet, rather backward, country town before its discovery by the tourists and the speculators.

6   So-called from its position on one side of the Square, on another side of which until 1859 the old Town Hall stood, the Square House is arguably the most prestigious building to have been lost in the town this century. At one time owned by a brewer with a chain of public houses along the south coast, it was demolished in 1959 after suffering a period of neglect. In the cellars were discovered a network of tunnels and storage chambers, implicating it in the smuggling trade so prevalent in the previous century. Adjacent is the brewery and the great stone arch erected in 1891 by Strong's, replacing earlier wooden gates. From this evidence the photo-graph can be dated between that time and 1905 when the tramlines appeared. The arch was in turn removed during the last war to facilitate the entrance of munitions vans to the yard behind. Note the ap-pearance of Taylor's Creamery, opposite.

Christchurch.

7   The camera has turned a few degrees to the right, drawing our attention to Burt's Carrier van come to a halt in front of Ye Olde George Inn. Dating from about 1908, this card captures a moment in time for James Burt, son of Cornelius, who commenced the business in 1864. Incredibly, Burts were still advertising just before the outbreak of the last war. The cart travelled daily from Purewell Cross through Southbourne and Bournemouth to Poole, returning from there at 3 p.m. The horses and carts were kept in stables in Wick Lane. Taylor's Creamery, a thriving offshoot of the dairy farm at Latch Farm, was also the town's first telephone call office in 1890 for the Western Counties Telephone Company.

19   CHRISTCHURCH. — High Street. — LL.

8   Slightly further up the High Street; this Mallett postcard dates from about 1903, just before Arthur Mallett gave up his photographic business in Church Street, to be replaced by the equally talented George Moss. Later occupants were C.D. Venning and G.N. Futcher – both photographers. Mallett advertised in 1898: '1,000 photographic views of the neighbourhood, including some of the Country Mansions around Christchurch': what a superb record of the town that would make now. This view shows the enclosed feel to the High Street created by the partial closure of the road at the far end by the Brewery House. On the right the fine wrought-iron frontage of Tuckers grocery stores can be made out, and opposite Ferrey's Drapery has received its 1899 third storey.

Mallett, Photo

High Street — Christchurch

Christchurch

9 This is a view in about 1920 of the shops on the eastern side of the High Street as far as Millhams Street. In the centre is the Ship Hotel (occasionally Millhams Street was known as 'Ship Lane'), an ale house since the late eighteenth century although originally the premises of a goldsmith, according to the deeds. Burnie's was a reputable outfitter's ('People's Clothier' says the signboard), beyond which is Cane and Galbraith, which styled itself 'The Christchurch Furniture Stores', selling furniture 'suitable for cottage or mansion', plus bedding purifying and linoleum fitting services. On the other side of the Ship, George Hill and Son, China Stores, where domestic requirements could be completed with 'glass, china and earthenware of every description, including Goss models of the Norman tower of the Priory, with descriptive notes'. All except Burnie's remain today.

10 The Country House Tea Rooms: although this business was transferred to Church Street early in the First World War and carried on trading there at least until the Second World War, this postcard shows its interior when it was situated on the east side of the High Street, around 1905. Throughout most of this period it was run by a Mrs Berkeley, who seems to have furnished it like a typical Edwardian domestic sitting room, complete with richly patterned carpets and wicker furniture. Newspapers and crockery are strewn around informally, creating a cluttered but cosy atmosphere. Interestingly, there was a Country House Inn in the middle of the road at Bargates until around 1856, so the name has been familiar to many Christchurch generations.

The Country House Tea Rooms, Christchurch.

11 This appears to be the same building as the previous card: Number 35 High Street, now, in 1922, in the ownership of The International Tea Company's Stores Limited. Although the card is marked 'Christmas' on the reverse, there is no evidence of any festivity. The windows are full of adverts for Mitre Margarine, Pure Coffee and Pure Cocoa Essence. The gentleman on the right is a Mr Eric Bryant. Trading methods undoubtably changed, but the grocery company remained until relatively recently – appearing in local guides as late as 1974. The little shop was demolished when an entrance was formed into the new Saxon Square in the 1980s.

12 Further towards Fountain Corner, this 1900 scene is hard to pinpoint today. In fact, the discerning eye would pick out only the upper window in the centre shop as still unaltered. Payn's, which was replaced about 1960 by Barclays Bank, was a 'Linen and Woollen Draper and Silk Mercer', also taking on any business that came along by way of furnishing funerals. The premises were known as Manchester House, probably on account of the cotton goods sold as well as the other fabrics. The shop on the left of Manchester House now abuts the service entrance to Saxon Square, which also accounts for the disappearance of the remaining buildings on the extreme left. The elevations are very similar to those of Bargates, which was until the 1958 bypass a continuation of the High Street.

13   On the opposite side of the street, the present Library around 1900, built as a house in 1844 for the solicitor James Druitt, a major figure in Christchurch: Mayor several times, a Guardian of the Poor, and J.P. At his death in 1904 he owned several shops in the town, much land locally and many cottages in poorer areas of Christchurch and Bournemouth. His son, Herbert, became the town's foremost and most distinguished local historian and used the house as one of his many stores for his books and other collections. Herbert Druitt fought passionately during the war to retain the railings in front of the property, but they were requisitioned for scrap iron. The Masonic Hall alongside was constructed for the Lodge of Hengist in 1837; the magnificent doorway apparently came from Winkton House.

14 The town's Post Office. Built in 1914, its entire ground-floor frontage with the quaint window was removed in 1960 and the building now houses electricity showrooms. On the first floor was the telephone exchange: the operator and her husband lived in the top floor flat and had to be available most hours. As far as the postal side of the service, a 1930s local rag mag referred to it somewhat mischievously: 'Here, thanks to the broad-mindedness of the postmaster, any casual visitor may handle the mailbags and take one away as a souvenir!' Cuff's, next door, claimed to be 'the oldest established Corn and Forage trade, Coal and Coke Merchant and Miller'. This attractive shop supplied a variety of fodder requirements; 'Linseed and cotton cake always on hand.' In 1920 Cuff's and the building adjoining it were replaced by the Midland Bank.

15 Getting closer to the junction with Barrack Road, this 1934 view of this (western) side of the High Street gives a closer view of Brewery House, removed in 1954 to widen the road. Note the clock on the side, advertising the brewery, Framptons, so attractively, the entrance to which is indicated by the arrow. Beyond this building is the landmark Antelope Hotel, forming the southernmost tip of the Pit Site and the junction of Barrack Road and Bargates. This was demolished for similar reasons in 1957. Nearer to us, the graceful eighteenth-century Bow House, another Brewery property, survived 1970s calls for its demolition. The remaining building, on the left, is the Excelsior Motor Garage, also owned at this time by the Frampton Brothers. It continued under different ownership until the early 1980s and the site is currently occupied by a supermarket.

16 Should business or curiosity lead you to approach the entrance to Frampton's Brewery, through the open gates you would have seen the extensive range of brewery buildings, most of which date back to its early Victorian origins as the Christchurch Steam Brewery, owned by George Olive Aldridge, who lived in the Elms at the corner of Pound Lane and the High Street. In 1907 the Frampton brothers, local men, acquired it, which was probably not long after the intriguing brewery tower was constructed. Hammertons bought the business in 1934, then it went to Watneys in 1951. Neither company used the tower and inevitably it was pulled down in 1955. Note the 'Wine and Spirits' sign on the lantern. All these remaining buildings, so full of character, made way for the Bank Close car park in the 1970s.

17 A glance down the High Street in 1934, showing the Midland Bank which replaced Cuff's, on the right. In the foreground is the side elevation of the Brewery House with the edge of the window display of Miss Simpson's shop – Milliner and and Costumier. Mr Proctor's tempting 'Home Made Sweets' shop is next door, then Mr Cathcart's greengrocery.

18   Looking back down to the way we have come. This photograph, which has appeared as a postcard, was taken by George Moss from an upper window of the Antelope Hotel, probably in 1904. In the foreground can be seen the lamp on the top of the fountain: this was erected just a couple of years previously as a tribute to Samuel Bemister, seven times Mayor of the town. It was designed to suit the needs of both animals and mankind: a miniature moat around the base kept the dogs happy; horses could use the water in the trough; whilst the people availed themselves of a tin cup on a chain! Moved from this site to the Quomps to be out of the way of those demanding machines which drink petrol rather than water, it has been restored in the last few years and returned to within site of its original home, at the bottom of Bargates.

19 Pound Lane, a narrow and rather humble row of cottages leading from the High Street corner to – well, it would be to Saxon Square these days, but originally it meandered on to a dairy farm. Much more ancient than the brick cottages is the stone-walled pound from which it got its name – a feature of this typical country town for centuries; the purpose was to keep stray livestock in, of course. An enterprising cottager has placed a sign against it, bringing the casual passers-by attention to 'Mill Stream Nursery. Blue door in wall on right.' Many of these cottages had long gardens and were to all intents and purposes small market gardens. All, whether medieval or Victorian, were swept away in 1958 for the bypass, the underpass to which is on the site of this picture.

20 Those cottages that were glimpsed in the previous picture at the end of Pound Lane can be seen at close quarters here, looking neat and re-spectable, although long be-fore they were demolished this area of the town had de-teriorated. That they look so spruce in this picture, with white-scrubbed steps, well-painted joinery and roofs in perfect order, suggests it may have been taken in the early years of the twentieth century. They were called St George's Square.

21 We are now just a few yards into Barrack Road, looking back to the High Street, where the upper storey of the shop formerly a private house called the Elms can just be seen above the tops of the cars in this 1937 photograph. The half-timbered Fountain Hotel stands at the corner of Soper's Lane: it was built in 1907 and boasted a billiards room, smoke rooms, a large club room and a tea garden. There are no gardens in sight there today! On the left the plain-looking building used as a poster hoarding was once the stables of the Cross Keys public house, the edge of which can just be seen. These last buildings were the Barrack Road side of the so-called 'Pit Site', all of which is now occupied by the Fountain roundabout.

22 Modern commercial considerations do not flatter this pleasing 1832 building, which now has to pay its way as an amusement arcade. Built by Joseph Hannaford, a builder who was often called on for repairs at the Priory Church, on land belonging to the Mary Magdalen Hospital, it subsequently became the home and business of John Cooper Bemister in the late Victorian period. He claimed to be 'the oldest Established Coal Business in Christchurch'. Between the wars it became an unemployment office, and has also done service as a sports pavilion for the adjacent recreation ground. Once surrounded by well-kept gardens of its own, it lost much of its original frontage to road widening in 1960. Despite these tribulations, its exterior has survived well; only a string of coloured lights and gaudy paint make it look different from this 1934 photograph.

23 Just further along the edge of Barrack Road Recreation Ground, and photographed in the same year: the difference in this scene and the view today is dramatic, largely because Barrack Road is now a roaring four-lane highway. More subtle but equally visually detrimental changes have occurred: many less trees are to be seen today and all the railings went for the war effort. The car near the direction sign is passing Magdalen Lane, in the vicinity of which the Hospital of St Mary Magdalen survived as a 'leper' colony for hundreds of years until about the late seventeenth century, and it still functions as a charity today, but for the poor rather than the afflicted. On the other side of the road, the Christchurch Lawn Tennis Club offered two hard and three grass courts, now built over.

24 Although faded, this 1880 photograph has great rarity value as a group picture of Royal Horse Artillery men at their ease in front of the Guard House at the Barracks. The sentry box on the left and the small dog in front are of especial intereSt The Barracks have a long and fascinating history going back to about 1792, but in 1925 the local paper observed that 'The spacious buildings and yards which once resounded with the noise of horses, limbers and troops, are now lying empty and practically un-used'. Not much later, the site developed into an experimental bridging establishment and later still became famous as the birthplace of the Bailey bridge. The Guard House, now experiencing the new and rather incongruous surroundings of a retail park, is Grade 11 listed, and a new use for it is being sought.

25 Christchurch Barracks again. A Venning photograph, which dates it to approximately the 1920s, although the gun has been identified as a 60-pounder BL Mark 1, a type which predates the First World War. The parade of field artillery, with eight horses and a field gun, is taking place on the parade ground with the military hospital in the background to the right; the gun carriage sheds at right angles to this; and the rear of the guard house just projecting next to that. There is a group of children watching in front of the hospital. This view today is of the edge of a new housing estate, the entrance to it where the gun carriage sheds used to front Barrack Road.

26 The upper end of Barrack Road about 1920. The rudimentary state of this main road is remarkable: surfaced only with bare earth, it must have become impassable in heavy rain. The mixture of traffic modes is of great interest: bicycles dominate, a farm cart and a motor car complete the quiet scene. The shop on the left is at the corner of Beaulieu Road and is now a fast-food outlet; opposite, the Victorian house is now the Laurels Rest Home.

Barrack Road, Stourvale. 404.

27　We have now travelled as far up Barrack Road as it originally went: it became a track after this, not having much else to go to. We are standing on the ancient stone Iford Bridge, gazing at the lovely village of Iford, which was part of Christchurch until 1931. This card is postmarked 1908, so the eventual obliteration of this beauty spot is mercifully some way off. The ladies are pausing at the river's edge; the strong metal rail prevented horses from drowning in the deep holes in the bed of the Stour at this point. Beyond Old Bridge Lane and the farm buildings can be seen the untamed heath upon which more of Bournemouth was soon to arise; the next port of call from here in this direction was the small village of Pokesdown.

28 Glancing across to the right as we remain on the bridge at Iford, the village cottages line Water Lane opposite the exit from the bridge. Although there is no hint of it in this idyllic scene, the road over the bridge to Christchurch was soon afterwards no place to stand and contemplate. Even in 1907, a traffic census counted 443 vehicles (though few of these would have been motorised) in a 12-hour period. The bridge was just 18-ft wide. Traffic intensity reached crisis point in the 1920s: local Christchurch people would regard it as an afternoon's fun watching the chaos created by traffic vying for priority on the bridge. A harassed RAC officer was stationed at the Christchurch end to attempt to keep order.

A new bridge was built in the early 1930s, restoring Iford's tranquillity – only the cottages had all been swept away by 'progress', leaving the old bridge to radiate its charm to new brick.

Iford Village.

29   Back to the centre of the town, and a more urban scene. This is the Pit Site (the name refers to gravel extraction) on the Bargates side. Although it was taken in the 1950s soon before entire demolition to make way for the bypass, these houses would not have changed in appearance since the preceding years. They had for a long time been regarded as crowded and sub-standard. They became increasingly marooned in an island of traffic and now nothing remains of them except the traffic island – the Fountain roundabout.

30 The bypass also spelled the end in 1958 of this section of lower Bargates, opposite the Pit Site. A particularly sad loss is the central building, variously known as Gould's House (after an earlier occupant, a recluse who left £80,000 to charity), West End House (the name for this part of Bargates), and the Georgian House (although it was probably seventeenth century). In the 1930s it was used as an antique shop, and the owners proudly welcomed visitors inside to admire the old building's interior features.

The lane alongside this house was Spring Gardens, another humble row of cottages similar to Pound Lane and similarly blessed with large garden plots.

31 This Edwardian postcard of the Baptist Tabernacle at the corner of Beaconsfield Road and Bargates seems to depict it almost as it is today, but in fact the frontage has been 'modernised'. It is not the first Baptist church on the site: an earlier one constructed in 1875 became very dilapidated not many years later and an appeal was launched to replace it, which was achieved about 1900. It had then been augmented by an attached school for 100 children. The driving force behind this improvement and of the church for many years after was the Rev. R.J. Peden, a native of County Durham, who arrived in the town in 1896. He also served as secretary for special services at the workhouse.

Baptist Tabernacle, Christchurch.

M.J.R.B. 1180.

32 Dated 1917 on the reverse, this postcard shows a snowbound Christchurch such as we rarely see in recent times. Taken from just in front of the British Legion hall, it shows a street scene barely altered sixty years on. Beaconsfield Road is in the middle left, with the Conservative Club of 1912 prominent on the right. In the centre distance the low roof of some of the Silver Street cottages, part of the Pit Site, project into the road. The Pit Site streets are now the site of a car park. This part of Bargates, as far as Silver Street, was known as West End. In the right foreground two cottages occupy another site which has been redeveloped.

Other changes time has brought are the removal of the tramlines, the posts and wires of which are clearly visible, and the disappearance of front boundary walls.

33 Just before the railway bridge on the Bargates side, at Fairmile, Light and Company's Timber Yard brought in their raw material, enormous tree trunks from the New Forest, over the bridge, by horse and cart or steam-wagons, for processing here. In the vast sheds a huge band-saw reduced the mighty trunks to usable timber. On the right is the foreman, a Mr Rymer, and seated on the right is Alec Dennett. Fourth from the back on the left is Thomas Jonas, a saw-doctor. Second from left at the back is Dick Russell. This photograph, by George Moss, dates from about 1910; the firm went into liquidation in the lean years of the 1930s. A cement works continues the industrial use of this site at present.

34 Latch Farm Cottage in Fairmile. This charming dwelling near the fire station gladdened the eye for very many years, until it was condemned and demolished in 1968. It was probably one of the oldest houses in Christchurch and had cob walls 18" thick. Fairmile was once characterised by thatched cottages: at the beginning of the twentieth century there were a dozen similar ones in the road, the mud to build them said to have come from the Pit Site. Latch Farm Cottage would not have met current building regulation standards today, and the social services would have been appalled to know that a family of fourteen children was successfully raised here within living memory.

35 This is the Master's House, for over sixty years the hub of the town's workhouse in Fairmile Road, which became Christchurch Hospital when the health service was created in 1948. In this photograph dating from the early 1920s, the Master, Mr Bill Morgan, stands with his wife and son at the imposing Jumpers Road entrance; the nurse is Sister Jefferson. Although these institutions were naturally dreaded, the Christchurch Union Workhouse displayed a compassionate attitude and earned a well-deserved good reputation. By the time of this picture, the care of the elderly and sick had already become a major function of this workhouse. The buildings, dating from 1881, were exceptionally solidly constructed, and well cared for (partly by the inmates). The entire 19th-century core of the complex, which extended to six acres, has almost all recently been demolished, although the Master's House was saved.

36　During the First World War, first one and then two infirmaries at the workhouse were requisitioned as a Red Cross hospital, eventually to become the largest VAD hospital in Hampshire. The patients came straight from the front, travelling by ship to Southampton and then by train to Christchurch Station. Here they were met by a volunteer ambulance brigade – Miss Starkey's Motor Ambulances – and Mr Lord's 'Stretcher Bearer Corps', and brought to the hospital. In this postcard, soldiers are being cared for by Red Cross nurses, who were from the two local VAD divisions under the command of Mrs Louden and Miss Ricardo. Every week the local paper appealed for supplies from the public, from bandages to cigarettes. As the numbers of wounded grew, temporary wards were constructed, and all given 'Empire' names: South Africa, Malta, Canada; also 'Kitchener' and 'Haig'.

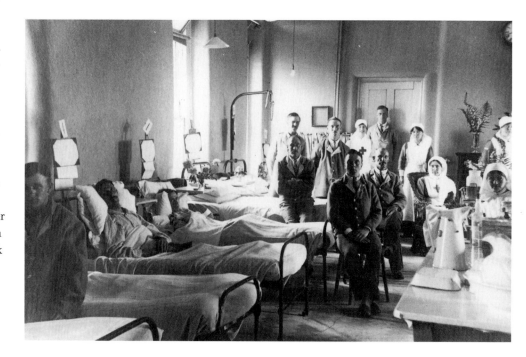

37   Just beyond the borough boundary, Blackwater Ferry is included here because it was a crossing point for Christchurch people to reach Holdenhurst over the Stour and a much frequented beauty spot. The boatman operated it by an overhead rope system. In the early Victorian era the cottage was once the Jolly Sailor Inn, but in the Edwardian period of this picture the only beer for sale was ginger beer – or a cup of tea could be enjoyed instead for about 4d. Here, a group of people appear to have cycled to the ferry: their machines leaning on the fence behind them. Disaster struck in the First World War: the boat and rope were caught up in a flood by a dislodged tree trunk and swept away, putting an end to the ferry operation. The cottage with its beautiful blanket of thatch became derelict and was pulled down some years later. Now the river is crossed a little further on from this point by the Bournemouth Spur Road.

BLACKWATER FERRY.

38 Christchurch at one time had many thatched buildings. Fire and fashion has accounted for the demise of most of them. These cottages are in Wick Lane, as they appeared in the 1930s. Just before the Second World War the thatch was replaced with concrete tiles, but if you inspect them today you will see other changes. The left-hand one is a gift shop; a bay window has replaced the downstairs sash. The centre cottage has long been occupied by an estate agent; this one also has a ground-floor bay, and a portico over the door. The right-hand cottage, with the bicycle leant against it, has also been altered, being built out at the street with a bay window to the pavement level and a chunky canopy over. The modern commercial use often hides the humble domestic origins of town centre buildings.

39 No book with Christchurch views is complete without one of the famous Wick Ferry. In use for hundreds of years for entirely functional reasons as a means of crossing the Stour before Tuckton Bridge was built, it became a popular visitor attraction with the advent of tourism. The Miller family owned it for many years until 1903; later Mr J. Edmunds was the operator, and in 1928 advertised the attraction as having: '...every facility – boating, refreshments, accommodation, car parking, camping grounds etc. ... Unspoiled by the builder and delightfully rural,' it ends ominously.

The original jetty with its little thatched shelter shown here was on the Wick side of the river. On the far side the landing stage is now part of Manor Parcs Holiday Village. This picture also features the ferry tea boat, where you could get 'plain teas', or collect 'tea baskets' if you had hired your own boat.

CHRISTCHURCH. — Wick Ferry. — LL.

40 Castle Street corner at the turn of the century, dominated by the building now occupied by Lloyds Bank. This building has been used as a bank continuously since 1836, when it opened as the Wilts and Dorset Bank, the head office of which had opened in Salisbury the previous year. It became Lloyds in 1918 following the amalgamation of the two banks. Until the creation of the post of Borough Treasurer in 1936, this bank acted as the Borough Council's honorary treasurer. It has hardly altered, except for the upper storey being painted to resemble stone.

41 On the other side of Castle Street, the premises of T.H.Barnes, 'Cash Draper', advertising in 1898: 'Noted Calicos in four ranges ... Latest styles in millinery always on view in the showroom ... Cash Price and Goods marked in Plain Figures – One Price only. No long credits and no discounts.' Next door is the slightly more customer-friendly looking shop of W. Spickernell, who promoted himself in the same year as a man of many talents – upholsterer, cabinet maker, and furniture dealer, also the agent for Peace furniture remover. This turn-of-the-century photograph shows clearly the stone-flagged pavement, which once extended round the corner into Church Street. A section remains today around The Old George Inn and beyond. Barnes' shop has barely changed, but Spickernell's has had a timbered shopfront where the pretty bay is. Note the carved panel in front of the upper windows, left perhaps by a previous business.

42 A later view – probably in the early 1930s – including the Old Court House. Spickernell's shop looks the same and has an 'Antiques' sign; Barnes' is now R.W. Hill's, basketmaker and wicker worker. Outside the Old Court House hangs the sign saying 'The Noted Pork Shop', for this was Queenie Scott's pork butcher's shop. It was renowned for her homemade hand-linked sausages and for her cleanliness. The business seems to have ceased in the late 'thirties; when the shop was refitted the joists were seen to be made from ships' timbers. Remnants of a row of meat hooks can still be seen attached to the attractive Victorian frontage of this fine medieval building.

5859. The Old Court House, Christchurch.

43 An Edwardian view of a much-photographed Christchurch scene: the old Town Bridge over the Avon, with Bridge House on the right. During the renovation of the bridge in 1937, a fascinating assortment of objects was recovered. These included two Neolithic flint arrowheads, old clay pipes, a Cromwellian spur and a Roundhead officer's cap badge, and a quantity of coins from the reigns of Queen Anne to George IV. Also found and promptly reported to the police were a quantity of loaded cartridges and a rifled domestic safe! Whether the undated human remains found were also reported to the authorities the newspaper account did not reveal.

The Bridge, Christchurch.

44 Castle Street continues into Bridge Street: here it is in the Edwardian period, making its curvaceous way towards Waterloo Bridge in the distance. The passers-by may not have known that the tall, Georgian building in the centre was for many years the town's customs house. The Revenue men had the hopeless task of patrolling the coastline for miles around; from the dormer window they could keep a watch on Hengistbury Head, a frequently used landing spot for contraband. The smuggling trade had died out by the middle of the nineteenth century.

45 This postcard view taken from Waterloo Bridge offers a rare glimpse of the cluster of agricultural buildings on Convent Meadow, known then as now as Avon Wharf. In view are stables and sheds and probably the forge; there were also a wheelwright's shop, a mason's workshop and a granary. These were constituent elements of the Christchurch Monumental Works – a business offering a huge range of goods and services, particularly headstones, but also coal and timber, garden supplies (flowerpots, wheelbarrows, edgings), ladders, cabinet-making, upholstery and under-taking. After the owner, John Preston, died, the site was sold in 1910 and most of these buildings were adapted to their new use as a thriving boatyard.

46   Purewell in flood, Denmark Place on the right with the Wesleyan Chapel projecting beyond. Floods in the town were regular and often dramatic, necessitating the roads being used as waterways, as here. This picture may date from one of the worst inundations, that of 1915, but other notable ones were 1867, 1883, and even as late as 1979. A witness to the 1883 floods climbed the Priory tower and saw a wilderness of water extending for miles up the Avon valley, 'like a great inland sea'. On such occasions it was common for Stoney Lane, Bridge Street and Purewell to be under as much as a couple of feet of water. The cause may have been the rivers being choked with weeds and silt; recent extensive flood protection works have made this misery another thing of the paSt

47 Further down Purewell, looking towards Purewell Cross and apparently taken in the 1920s. Little has changed in this scene, but all the land behind the Salisbury Arms which was once Pritchards' prize-winning nursery, the front wall of which is visible in the foreground, has been built on. Beyond the public house the Roman Catholic Chapel of 1868 can be glimpsed. There is very little to indicate that the road through Purewell was the main road to Southampton and London.

48   On the boundary between Stanpit and Mudeford. Argyle House, the first house in Mudeford, has a projecting sign advertising 'Argyle Library'. It is now a post office, and the front door at its corner is removed; otherwise the view is largely unaltered, apart from the modern street furniture. Francis Bernard Argyle was a nineteenth-century shoemaker but also a collector of curiosities and an antiquary. He gave the land on which the Roman Catholic Church at Purewell was built. He died in 1888, after which other land he owned in the area was sold for development.

288   MUDEFORD. CHRISTCHURCH

49 Looking back towards Christchurch centre from the same spot: but a few years later: the library sign, though not its bracket, has gone and the shop has changed hands. From about the First World War through the 1920s, Miss Eliza Clark ran this corner shop as a draper and grocer famed for her sherbet dabs. On the right is Mudeford Recreation Ground. Throughout most of the nineteenth century this area was called the 'sand waste', on account of it being used as a source of sand for sprinkling on stone-flagged floors, as the custom was. It was taken around the cottages by a man with a donkey cart. When this practice died out the land was laid out as a public park at the expense of a local benefactor, Mrs Maberley of Avonmouth House; this was completed by 1889.

50   The Avonmouth Hotel was originally known as Mudeford House, but changed its name to Avonmouth House when acquired in 1871 by General and Mrs Maberley, generous local benefactors, principally remembered for donating the land and the building costs of Stanpit Village Room, opened in 1887. The house and contents were sold in 1922: 'Freehold Marine Estate', the particulars said, going on to list the appointments, which included a cottage, stabling for five horses, a coach house and jetty, plus kitchen garden and piggeries; all in all nearly five acres. The contents included a grand piano, four grandfather clocks, numerous valuable oil paintings and a two-seater motor car. In this postcard, much of the surrounding farmland yet remains, but since then it has all been developed.

4090.   AVONMOUTH HOTEL, MUDEFORD, NR. CHRISTCHURCH.

51 This is the view from Chichester Way, which leads to Mudeford Quay. On the left is a house known as the Lawns, and straight ahead is a block of early eighteenth-century houses known as the Moorings. This group has had a chequered past: the left-hand half of the white portion was for many years known as the Sandford Hotel in the mid-Victorian period, and the centre portion was Sandford House. The dark section was Stratford Villa. The white sections became the Moorings Guest House and Tea Lounge about 1890 and traded as a hotel until the 1960s. The whole group is now private houses. Between the Lawns and the Moorings is a house known as The Staithe. The Lawns was demolished in 1967 to create another access road to Mudeford Quay.

291 MUDEFORD, CHRISTCHURCH

52 Standing in front of The Moorings, and looking towards Avon Beach: the Staithe is now on the right: in the mid-Victorian period this attractive building was a lodging house, but in 1947 was converted into flats. Since this postcard view, the ground floor has been extended forwards in keeping with the original. The pillar box is of particular interest and merit as it is one of the oldest in the country. Dating from about 1860, it has fluted columns on the sides. It has since been moved out of the way of the traffic! The lofty buildings on the left were known as the White House Stables, and were converted coach houses. Despite protests, they were removed in 1976 – as usual, the 'motor monstrosities' were the culprits. 'What was to say future generations will not find beauty in the Mudeford coach houses?' prophetically enquired an enlightened councillor at the time.

53 A view of the enigmatic Mudeford Quay not obtainable today on account of the Highcliffe Sailing Club headquarters and the lifeboat station intervening. From left to right: the Haven House Inn, early Victorian; Haven House, probably Dutch-built, seventeenth century; coastguard cottages, early nineteenth century. This group of buildings between them tell an immense amount of history: of daring landings of contraband; of skirmishes with the Revenue men which in 1784 left an officer dead; of the legitimate salmon fishing in the Run beyond; and of the lonely but alert Customs officers guarding the harbour entrance. The fishermen and their families in this postcard look innocent enough, staring at the photographers curiously in a world where tourism had barely been invented. Where they stand are today the slipways of pleasure craft.

54 When this postcard was printed the photographer would have had to peer through a thick surround of trees; now this lovely eighteenth-century house is obscured by static caravans. Sandhills was constructed for Sir George Henry Rose, a diplomat and personal friend of King George III, whose visit to him here put Mudeford on the map.

A sale brochure of 1871 ascribes to it 'a position of unsurpassed beauty', which is unusually accurate for an estate agent! After the last war, the house ceased to be a gracious residence of the privileged, and was requisitioned by the local authority to ease the acute post-war housing shortage. Later it provided overflow classroom accommodation for the local primary school. It is currently used as the centre of a holiday business.

"SANDHILLS" MUDEFORD

55   Demolished in 1957, this impressive house commanded a fine position at the northern edge of Mudeford. Known as Bure Homage, it was built around 1830 and surrounded by some 30 acres of ornamental gardens, bisected by a little stream (the Bure); beautiful grounds that the resident Ricardo family readily permitted local cricket teams to use, and where many a Mudeford fete was enjoyed. The heyday of the country squirearchy with their host of servants was drawing to a close, however. The Ricardos left in 1939, not long after the grand house was requisitioned for the war effort. The deterioration that this inevitably entailed left it in a poor state of repair and beyond economical use. The grounds which once boasted tiger lilies, carnations, greengages and medlar trees soon became plots for bungalows.

56 Ice House Hill, a name that has fallen out of use, referred to an ice house built for Nea House, which graced Nea Meadows until during the Second World War. The entrance gates to this Georgian house stood near the junction of Hinton Wood Avenue and Nea Road; close by the underground ice cavern supplied the resident Cameron family with frozen game or pure ice. The narrow mud track and the tangle of trees do not remind one of Highcliffe as it is now, but Nea Meadows has managed to preserve a rural element in this built-up part of the borough.

57 Verdant vegetation is once again prominent in this Victorian view of Highcliffe village. The picture was taken from close to the Globe Inn, looking eastwards, and can only easily be identified by the building on the left past the thriving hedge and trees. This marks the corner of Bucehayes Close. On the right-hand side, the two Victorian houses remain, looking much as they do here, but the buildings beyond have been replaced with modern shops. The row of chimneys poking above the leaves on the other side belong to cottages now converted to shops. Gone, of course, is the encroaching roadside vegetation, which today might offend the local authority and the highway board, as well as the local chamber of trade! A pavement is considered to be more appropriate today.

58 By the look of the car parked behind the tea house, this postcard appears to date from the 1930s, and shows a rudimentary refreshment room apparently situated where the car park is today. As can be seen, the cliff edge was more natural in appearance in those days, and it was a favourite destination for blackberry pickers. An advert of 1933 referring to the Beach Tea House, describes Highcliffe beach as 'The Fairyland of the Sea'.

HIGHCLIFFE-ON-SEA, THE TEA HOUSE.

59 It is 1905: a superb photograph captures the workmen pausing for the camera before they recommence their task of laying the tram tracks across Tuckton Bridge. There is a wealth of detail: the horse with its cart and brasses; the toll house behind it; the workmen in shirtsleeves and the supervisors in suits. The replacement of the first bridge of 1883 was not universally welcomed: one observer complained bitterly of the trees that had been cut down, the riverbank sliced into, and the dreadful state of the roads. When the trams ceased in 1936, they were not lamented: 'Unwept, Unhonoured, and Unsung ... good riddance to the lumbering old tramcar,' said the newspaper, spitefully. The tram route from the bridge was down Stour Road, Bargates, the High Street and outer Church Street as far as the old Dolphin Inn, and must have brought much-needed mobility to many Christchurch people.

60 Five years later, this card shows a tram making use of the new bridge. It is crossing to Christchurch from the Bournemouth side; the toll bridge can be seen at the far end, together with some of the as yet undeveloped land just beyond. Note the conductor on the platform and the stairs curving up at the rear. It is a Number 51. To our eyes, the tram seems not to have deserved the description quoted in the previous card: the bridge, the tram posts and the tram itself have strong visual appeal that the modern equivalents cannot be compared with! A tram outing to Poole was considered quite a treat for Christchurch people early in the nineteenth century, and a welcome alternative to the ferry at Wick or the long journey to Iford to cross the Stour. Tuckton Bridge remained a toll bridge as late as 1943.

61 Tuckton was part of Christchurch until 1895; here we see an Edwardian card showing the boat house and the boats set out for hire, and on the river the tea-houses, which were sometimes converted steamers. An excursion to this spot was well advertised for visitors, and provided a range of boating facilities including canoes and punts, with instruction if needed. The photographer is standing just in front of the bridge on the Tuckton side, looking east along the river to the Priory in the distance; again the natural state of the river bank on the Christchurch side is noteworthy.

Tuckton Creek, Christchurch. 3754.

62 Winkton village was long the centre of a very old Christchurch cottage industry, that of glove-making, which was still providing employment as late as the 1880s. The occupants of this house here almost certainly never had to scrape a living in this way. Now Homefield School and today barely recognisable as the former Winkton Lodge, it was long connected with the Walcott family. The cedar on the left may have been the one planted by Admiral Walcott himself.

WINKTON LODGE HOTEL, CHRISTCHURCH, HANTS.

63 Hinton Admiral, an imposing eighteenth-century residence, built to replace an earlier mansion destroyed by fire in the previous century, and the seat of the Meyrick family which is a major landholder in the town and district, particularly of land and property in the historic centre, and also holds the title to the Lord of the Manor of Christchurch Twyneham, one of three manors bearing the name of Christchurch. Today, this house is much as the postcard depicts. It is not accessible to the public but the grounds are open once a year when the rhododendron woods are in full display.

Meet of New Forest Foxhounds at Hinton Admiral.

64 This event depicts the opening of the celebration of the coronation of King George V in 1911 when the New Zealand flag was hoisted, after which the crowd proceeded to the opening of Convent Walk. The postcard shows the Town Hall exceptionally clearly. To the rear of the frontage can be seen the hall that was added early in the 1900s, with a further extension behind, both of which made way for Saxon Square in the early 1980s. The Town Hall, now Grade II listed, was almost swept away in the name of that chimera, progress, in 1959. At the time, not much protest at its potential loss was voiced: it was the cost of the proposed replacement that raised strong objections.

65   Christchurch, remarked the local paper, has a 'reputation for doing things thoroughly'. The coronation celebrations were to have continued with a tea for 1,500 children followed by organised sports on the town's recreation ground in Barrack Road, but these had to be postponed for a week because of poor weather. Here we see part of the 'Merry-making of Olden Times': a ladies' tug-of-war. The recreation ground is all that is left of Portfield, an area of almost 300 acres of open arable land over which the borough residents had common rights. When it was enclosed in 1878 so that the town could expand, these rights were abolished, but this portion was awarded to the parishioners for 'recreation and exercise', a status which has been reinforced by its registration as a village green.

CORONATION FETES 1911 CHRISTCHURCH   29

66　This is a scene from National Gun Week in 1918, a fundraising exercise which produced £27,000 from the borough for the war effort. The mayoral car has stopped outside the Masonic Hall in the High Street, its occupant, the Mayor, William Tucker JP. The Tucker family owned the long-established provisions shop of that name in the High Street, where Alderman Tucker himself worked until 1909, although undertaking many public offices in addition. He had 'decided views which he was not afraid the express', said his obituary. He left a useful booklet reminiscing about local affairs beginning with his arrival here in 1844.

67 The Peace Celebrations of July 1919. This was another occasion when the elders of the town excelled themselves in creating a packed programme of spectacular events, and were rewarded by the enthusiastic support of the populace. Here, a procession which would have included decorated vehicles, pedestrians, tradesmen and draught animals in fancy costume, are just reaching the High Street from their start at Mudeford after the judging. Note the Royal Navy ensign. The day was filled with events — massed bands, a fete, a dinner, culminating in a walk along the Convent Walk which had been illuminated to create 'a fairyland spectacle unequalled in Great Britain'; fireworks at Hengistbury Head and the National Anthem sung in the Square at midnight.

68   One of the major events in the town, which was always well supported, was the annual Saturday and Sunday Hospital Sundays. These were set up to fund the voluntary hospitals and had nothing to do with Christchurch Hospital, which did not come into being until the NHS was created in 1948. This scheme was inaugurated in 1886 and supported not only the Royal Victoria Hospital in Boscombe but other institutions which benefited local people, such as the Mineral Water Hospital in Bath and the Eye Hospital at Southampton. Street and church collections were made, carnivals, firework displays, dances and concerts held, all of which made a major contribution to the income of such places. In this picture a float proclaims: 'Hello! Christchurch Calling! Grand Carnival Procession', but the date is indecipherable.

69 This pony and trap seems to be waiting patiently with its groom in Quay Road for its passenger. The passenger would be the Rev. T.H Bush, who purchased the Red House in 1886 after the pauper children occupying it were removed to the new workhouse recently constructed in Fairmile. This postcard view was taken from the front of that building with the churchyard behind. The carriage appears to be immaculate, with brass coach lamp and polished foot-rests. A whip is slotted into its holder ready for use should the need arise. The groom is spotless from his top hat to his leather boots.

70 These children proudly upholding their banner are members of one of the many temperance groups which flourished in the town at the end of the nineteenth century and well into the twentieth. They particularly targeted children: this group belongs to 'The Star of Liberty of the Independent Order of Rechabites', a branch of which was founded in the town in 1895. The children's section was known as the Snowdrop campaign, and met in the infants' schoolroom in Millhams Street (now the Lighthouse youth club) and also at the Wesleyan Chapel in Purewell. Other temperance groups included the Primrose League, the Church of England Temperance League (which met in the National Schoolrooms, in Wick Lane – now the Priory School), and the Blue Ribbon Gospel Temperance Union. Children were expected to 'sign the pledge' to abstain from drink.

71 A sailing match in the harbour. Christchurch Sailing Club was formed about 1874. In this postcard view, the clubhouse can be seen just behind the yacht on the left. Membership in 1908 cost 10s 6d for the gentlemen and just 5s for the ladies; the ladies were not, however, permitted any voting rights. Matches were held throughout the year for many classes of boat – some fifty were arranged for the year 1928 – but the culmination of the club year and a major event in the town's calendar became the annual August regatta. Rowing, swimming and sports as well as the sailing races were organised, accompanied by band music on the bandstand and followed by dancing at the King's Arms Hotel and fireworks set off from the castle mound. Illuminated boats would form a procession along the quayside as part of the culminating events.

Christchurch.   Priory and Sailing Match in the Harbour.   *as I am longing for a letter*

72 Inside the Priory School in the 1920s. A view of the earnest young scholars in the days when ceilings reached to the rafters, glass partitions divided the sexes, desks had inkwells and walls displayed School Board clocks and uplifting pictures. The school moved to this site from the High Street in 1867. Reminiscences from the end of the last century recall the feared cane, which when required the offender had to purchase from a fancy goods shop in the High Street! Tips to reduce the pain of the impact included rubbing the receiving end with orange peel. Children had enviable freedom in these days in many respects: the river close by being a source of free fun. Magic lantern shows at the Congregational Church and a trip to play on the wreck of Southbourne pier were amongst the innocent amusements recalled from these times.

73   The independent equivalent of the National Schools: the Congregational (now United Reformed) Church School was established as far back as 1830. The building in this picture of around 1923 is at the far end of Millhams Street; it was the infant section. The house for the mistress still survives, though sadly neglected in the late 1990s, and is known locally as 'the Doll's House'. Older children were taught in what is now the lecture hall of the church, used for W.I. markets today. 100 years ago the school roll was in the order of 300 and the minister, Daniel Gunn, instilled rigid discipline. The log books survive, and tell a familiar story of the struggle to enlighten young brains. With the opening of the Christchurch Infant School in Clarendon Road in 1929, this building ceased to have an educational function and it now accommodates a youth club, but faces an uncertain future.

74 The Christchurch Wednesday Football Team in 1907. Many well-known local names are recorded underneath: Butler, Troke, Ferrey, Gossling and Pope amongst them. The photograph celebrates their victory in the Bournemouth and District Wednesday League, which as its name suggests played each Wednesday. The League included Poole Wednesday, Wimborne Amateurs, Parkstone Wednesday, the Civil Service, Boscombe Institute, Bournemouth Rangers, Carter's United, and Wimborne St John's. The following year they did well too, apart from being late on account of missing the train taking them to a match at Meyrick Park!

Not long afterwards they achieved a spectacular score of 25-nil at home on the town recreation ground.

CHRISTCHURCH WEDNESDAY FOOTBALL TEAM.

WINNERS, 1906-7.

Bournemouth and District Wednesday League.

G. H. Ferrey,   J. C. Edmunds.   C. B. Ferrey (Capt.)   S. J. Gossling.   W. Remington.   R. H. Pope.   E. J. Cox,
        S. Butler.   J. Maidment.   J. Hunt.   W. Green.   C. Howe.
            F. Troke.   W. Evenden.   F. Ferrey.

75 Very much part of the legend and lore of Christchurch, this is the famed 'Ye Deluge' fire engine, probably on one of its outings in retirement to a local fete. The legend includes the inscription on the side about having attended the Great Fire of London, which was just the ironic humour of Charlie Burry, captain of the Fire Brigade. It was certainly ancient, perhaps as old as a date of the mid-eighteenth century ascribed to it in 1910. It made a big impression on those who attended an exhibition of antique fire appliances in London a few years earlier, as £100 was offered for it, but in Christchurch it became something of a laughing stock, so out of date had it become. 'It isn't worth 6d', was the local opinion. Only in 1926 was it allowed to rest, and survives still somewhere in the county museums service.

76 This collection ends with a typical Victorian Christchurch figure: Henry West Jenkins, walking on his lawn at Riversdale, the house he built for himself in Magdalen Lane in 1887. He built up from small beginnings the highly reputable building firm of Jenkins and Sons, which contributed high-quality workmanship to many of the new and old buildings of both this old town and its new neighbour, Bournemouth. They trained stonemasons, joiners, plumbers, glaziers, and all sorts of other skilled tradesmen and became greatly respected, so much so that they were selected to renovate Broadlands in Romsey in the 1960s. The firm survived for over 120 years. Mr Jenkins was also a stalwart of the Congregational Church, being a lay minister, and a Guardian of the Poor. The history of this town was largely made by such energetic figures as him – they set a fine example.